Contents

Any words shown in the text in bold, **like this**,
are explained in the Glossary.

Who was William Shakespeare?

William Shakespeare was a famous **playwright** and poet, who lived and worked in England 400 years ago. Many people today regard him as perhaps the greatest writer who has ever lived. His plays were very popular during his lifetime and their success made him a rich man. They are still performed today in different languages all over the world.

Full of colour

William Shakespeare had a brilliant imagination and captured the spirit of the times in which he lived. This was the **Elizabethan age**, when Elizabeth I was on the throne and England was enjoying one of the most important and exciting periods in its history. There were many voyages of discovery from European countries, including England, to distant lands such as India, the Far East and the Americas. The explorers brought back stories of places and adventures which inspired writers like Shakespeare.

Shakespeare wrote about human nature and how people behave towards each other. Today, actors, directors and theatre-goers all over the world believe Shakespeare's words have as much meaning in our own lives as they did centuries ago.

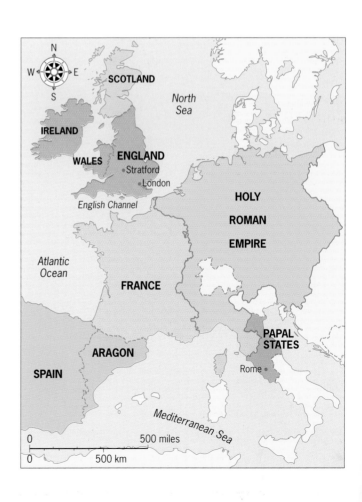

▶ This map shows the main kingdoms of Europe at the time Shakespeare was born.

The Life and W

WILLIAM SHAKESPEARE

Struan Reid

www.heinemann/library.co.uk
Visit our website to find out more information about Heinemann Library books.

To order:
☎ Phone 44 (0) 1865 888066
🖹 Send a fax to 44 (0) 1865 314091
💻 Visit the Heinemann Library Bookshop at www.heinemann/library.co.uk to browse our catalogue and order online.

First published in Great Britain by Heinemann Library,
Halley Court, Jordan Hill, Oxford
OX2 8EJ, part of Harcourt Education.
Heinemann is a registered trademark of Harcourt
Education Ltd.

© Harcourt Education Ltd 2003
First published in paperback in 2004
The moral right of the proprietor has been asserted.

Editorial: Lucy Thunder and Helen Cox
Design: Ron Kamen and Celia Floyd
Illustrations: Jeff Edwards and Joanna Brooker
Picture Research: Rebecca Sodergren
and Elaine Willis
Production: Séverine Ribierre

Originated by Ambassador Litho Ltd
Printed and bound in China by W K T

ISBN 0 431 14785 X (hardback)
07 06 05 04 03
10 9 8 7 6 5 4 3 2 1

ISBN 0 431 14792 2 (paperback)
08 07 06 05 04
10 9 8 7 6 5 4 3 2 1

British Library Cataloguing in Publication Data
Reid, Struan
Life and world of William Shakespeare
822.3'3

A full catalogue record for this book is available from
the British Library.

Acknowledgements

The Publishers would like to thank the following for
permission to reproduce photographs:
Art Archive p. **12**; Bridgeman Art Library/Ashmolean
Museum, Oxford p. **7**; Bridgeman Art
Library/Trustees of the National Museums & Galleries
of Merseyside p. **8**; Bridgeman Art Library/Scottish
NAtional Portrait Gallery, Edinburgh p. **13**;
Bridgeman Art Library/Private Collection p. **19**;
Bridgeman Art Library/British Library p. **28**; Camera
Press p. **6**; Camera Press/T. Spencer p. **10**; Corbis pp.
5, **9**, **11**, **21**, **23**, **29**; Corbis/Robbie Jack p. **25**;
Courtauld Institute of Art p. **17**; Dulwich Picture
Library p. **18**; Hulton Getty p. **16**; Mansell Collection
p. **20**; Mary Evans Picture Library p. **14**; National
Portrait Gallery p. **22**, **24**; National Trust p. **15**;
Shakespeare Birthplace Trust p. **27**; Shakespeare
Centre Library p. **26**.

Cover photograph of William Shakespeare,
reproduced with permission of Hulton Archive.

The Publishers would like to thank Rebecca Vickers
for her assistance in the preparation of this book.

Every effort has been made to contact copyright
holders of any material reproduced in this book. Any
omissions will be rectified in subsequent printings if
notice is given to the Publishers.

Disclaimer
All the Internet addresses (URLs) given in this book
were valid at the time of going to press. However,
due to the dynamic nature of the Internet, some
addresses may have changed, or sites may have
changed or ceased to exist since publication. While
the author and Publishers regret any inconvenience
this may cause readers, no responsibility for any such
changes can be accepted by either the author or the
Publishers.

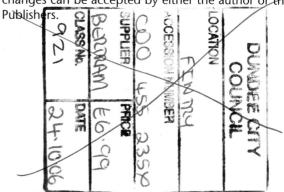

How do we know?

Very little is known about William Shakespeare's early life. Some people even think that the plays were really written by one of the other playwrights of the time. It is only when he became a successful playwright in London that his life becomes clearer.

Historians have managed to piece together a reasonably accurate picture of his life from records and documents that were kept at that time, and from letters that were written then and after his death. Perhaps the most useful source of information about the sort of person he really was are the words he himself wrote in his plays and poems.

▲ This is a portrait of William Shakespeare. No one is certain exactly what he looked like, but this is probably one of the more accurate pictures.

Key dates

1564	William Shakespeare is born
1582	William marries Anne Hathaway
1590	William moves to London at about this time
1591–1612	William writes *Romeo and Juliet* and other famous plays
1592–94	All the theatres in London are closed due to the **plague**
1603	Queen Elizabeth I dies
1613	William returns to live permanently in Stratford-upon-Avon
1616	William Shakespeare dies

The birth of a brilliant imagination

William Shakespeare was born in April 1564 in the town of Stratford-upon-Avon in Warwickshire. The exact date of his birth is not known, but church records show that he was **baptized** on 26 April. His parents were John and Mary Shakespeare.

A healthy boy

A few months after William was born, Stratford was overrun by a terrible outbreak of the **plague**. By September, one out of every fifteen people in Stratford was infected. Two hundred people eventually died from the disease. In those days it was very common for small children to die from all sorts of diseases, such as smallpox and influenza. Mary Shakespeare had already lost two baby daughters in this way, but William was a strong and healthy baby boy and he managed to survive.

▼ The house where William Shakespeare was born. It has been restored and is now a museum.

Successful businessman

William's father, John Shakespeare, was a 'wittawer' or leatherworker. He made gloves which he sold in the marketplace in the centre of Stratford. He was very successful at this business and became rich enough to buy some land and houses in the town. In 1557 he had married Mary Arden, the daughter of a wealthy farmer from the nearby village of Wilmcote.

In 1568, when William was four years old, his father was elected as **bailiff** of Stratford. He held this position for only a year, but altogether he served as a local government official for nearly 20 years. These appointments gave John Shakespeare and his family great importance and influence in Stratford.

▶ A pair of elaborate Elizabethan leather gloves like these could take weeks to make and so were very expensive to buy.

The plague

The plague often broke out in towns and cities during the reign of Elizabeth I. It was carried to people by fleas that lived on rats. The fleas carried the plague **bacteria** inside them and passed it on when they bit humans. **Infected** people suffered quick, but agonizingly painful, deaths. It was believed at the time that they could infect other people directly. Therefore, people were forbidden to visit each other for fear of spreading the disease from one household to another. When an outbreak ended, houses were aired and scrubbed clean and many of their furnishings were burned to try to stop the infection restarting.

Growing up in Elizabethan England

When William Shakespeare was born, Elizabeth I was on the throne of England. During her long reign, which lasted nearly 50 years, England became one of the richest and most powerful countries in Europe.

▲ This portrait shows Queen Elizabeth I in about 1574. She was one of the best-educated women of her time, and loved watching plays.

The royal court

Like most people at this time, William was brought up far away from London and Elizabeth I's dazzling royal **court**. In her many palaces she was attended by her ladies-in-waiting and by hundreds of **courtiers**, relatives and other people. They all depended on the queen for their own power and wealth. Painters, musicians and playwrights also flocked to Elizabeth's court. She loved listening to music and watching plays. Towards the end of her reign, William Shakespeare became one of her favourite **playwrights**.

Everyday life

Shakespeare's plays are full of examples of the way people lived at that time. For almost all people in Elizabethan England, life was hard and cruel. They lived in villages far away from the towns and cities. Large numbers of people worked farming the land. There were many poor people who often had very little to eat. **Plague** and other terrible diseases were common, so people often died young.

At this time, people were generally much more religious than they are today, and many went to church at least once a day. England was a **Protestant** country – during the reign of Elizabeth's father, King Henry VIII, the country had broken away from the **Catholic** Church in Rome. But even though most people were very religious, they also believed in **superstition** and **folklore** in which fairies and witches cast magic spells.

▲ **This is a modern replica of Sir Francis Drake's ship,** *Golden Hind*. **You can see the ship today in Brixham Harbour, Devon.**

An age of adventure

The Elizabethan age was a time of great exploration and adventure. Sailors and **navigators** like Sir Francis Drake, Humphrey Gilbert and Sir Walter Raleigh attended Elizabeth I's court. They all hoped to win her backing for new expeditions. In 1577, Sir Francis Drake left England to sail around the world on his ship, the *Golden Hind*. He returned nearly three years later having covered 57,935 km (36,000 miles). This spirit of adventure and activity comes across in many of Shakespeare's plays.

A boy in Stratford

When young William was growing up, Stratford was a thriving market town surrounded by rich farmland. About 1200 people lived there. Farmers brought their produce to town on market days – live animals and carts piled high with fruit, vegetables and grain. Among the animals were pigs and goats, the skins of which were used by William's father to make his gloves.

A growing family

When William was two years old, he was joined in the family by a baby brother, named Gilbert. Three years later, in 1569, a sister named Joan was born. Another sister, Anne, was born in 1571, but died seven years later. Then there were two more boys – Richard, born in 1574 and, finally, Edmund, born in 1580 when William was sixteen. As the oldest of the children, William would have been expected to set an example to his brothers and sisters and to help with their upbringing.

Off to school

William went to his first school when he was about five years old. From the age of about seven, he attended classes at the King's New School in Stratford, not far from the family home in Henley Street. He went six days a week for the next eight years. For most of the time William and the other boys at the school studied **Latin**. One master was usually in charge of about twelve boys and discipline was very strict.

▶ A view of one of the main streets in Stratford today, taken from the market square. Some of the houses remain the same as they were in Shakespeare's time.

Changed fortunes

At the end of 1576 or early 1577, when William was about 14 years old, his father got into **debt**. His glove-making business had not been going well for some years. He no longer attended council meetings and eventually, in 1586, he was voted out as an **alderman**. This change in John Shakespeare's fortunes must have had a great affect on William and all the family.

▶ This modern photograph shows schoolboys sitting in the classroom where William Shakespeare was taught.

Elizabethan school days

Most children in Elizabethan times received only a very basic education. Girls were usually educated at home by their mothers. From about the age of four or five, boys were sent to 'petty' school, where they were given religious studies and learned how to read and write. After about two years at school, they were expected to go out to work.

Marriage and fatherhood

William left school when he was about fifteen years old, but this part of his life is very unclear. He did not go on to study at university, as the sons of rich families would have done, but possibly began working for his father in his leather business. Some people believe that he became a schoolteacher, but if he did teach he probably worked as a private **tutor** to a rich family.

A family of his own

We do know that in 1582 William married Anne Hathaway, the eldest daughter of a local farmer. William was eighteen while Anne was eight years older than him. After their marriage, the couple lived with William's parents. In 1583 Anne gave birth to a baby daughter, named Susanna. Two years later, twins were born – a boy named Hamnet and another girl, named Judith.

Extra work

It was important for William to earn a living to support his growing family. As well as helping his father in the leather business, some people believe that William may also have joined a **company of actors** soon after he left school. At this time acting was frowned upon by most people, but at least it would have brought in some extra money.

▶ Anne Hathaway's cottage, near Stratford, which has been restored and is now kept as a museum.

On tour

Touring companies of actors often visited towns like Stratford and it is just possible that William joined one of them. The first company to visit Stratford came in 1568 when William's father was serving as **bailiff**. It is possible that he took his son to see some of their plays. They would probably have made a great impression on the young William.

▶ This painting shows a group of touring actors in Elizabethan times. The two boys at the front would probably have been apprentice actors.

Training to be an actor

Apprentice actors, or 'players' as they were known, started their training by playing small parts. The more experienced actors would teach them and also give them lessons in dancing and playing musical instruments. During a tour, apprentice actors were also expected to make themselves useful by doing odd jobs, like packing and unpacking the costumes and collecting the entrance money from the audience. All the apprentices would have been boys – there were no actresses in Elizabethan times.

London calls

S ome time after the birth of Hamnet and Judith, perhaps as early as 1587, William left Stratford for London. Mystery surrounds this stage of his life as well, and no one is certain why he left and what he went to do. Whatever it was that made him leave, William was to be away for most of the next 20 years. He left behind in Stratford his wife Anne and their three children and he would see them only occasionally over the following years.

The chance of success

If William was already a member of one of the touring **companies of actors**, he probably went to London with the group of actors he had joined in Stratford. London was the centre of English theatre and most young actors would have wanted to perform there. John Shakespeare's business was still struggling and William possibly decided that he was unlikely to be able to provide for his own wife and children, let alone his parents and brothers and sisters, if he stayed in Stratford. The chance of success in London was too much to turn down.

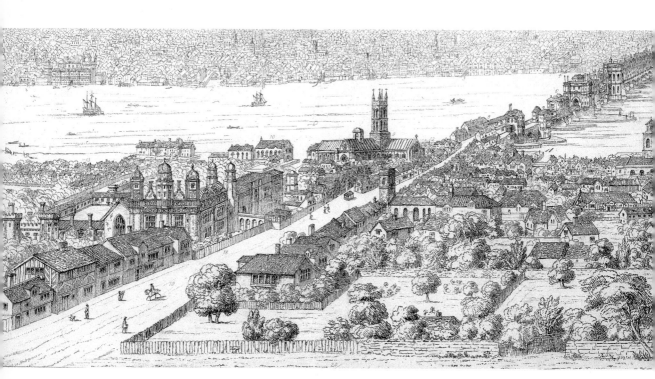

▲ This painting of London from 1548 shows the city of London as it looked in the 16th century. You can see London Bridge over the River Thames, and the old St Paul's Cathedral is in the distance.

Sixteenth-century London

London was one of the largest and most exciting cities in the world, with a bustling port and thousands of people living and working in its narrow streets. Rich **nobles** and **merchants** lived in splendour in great palaces and mansions. But most people lived in crowded, dirty houses.

Trading ships sailed up and down the River Thames that flowed through the city. They brought strange and wonderful goods to the port, while the merchants also brought back stories of the faraway lands they had visited.

▲ This is Sutton House, one of the few surviving Elizabethan buildings in London.

The heart of the city

Lying at the heart of the city of London was the great cathedral of St Paul's. The cathedral we see today was built on the site of the one that was there in William's time. This earlier cathedral was destroyed in the Great Fire of London (1666). St Paul's was London's main place of worship, while the area around it was one of the city's most important meeting places. Goods were sold from market stalls near by, while beggars and pickpockets took advantage of the people who came to buy.

A life in the theatre

To William and the hundreds of other young people who settled in London every year, the city must have seemed like the centre of the world. It would have taken him days to travel by horse from Stratford south to London. When he finally arrived there, his family and friends back in his home town must have felt very far away.

Finding his feet

William probably went to stay in an inn or lodging house on the south bank of the River Thames. Nearby was the Rose Theatre. He arrived in London at just the right time, when new theatres were being built and people were flocking to see plays. Even Elizabeth I loved watching plays, and she had her own **company of actors**.

Some historians believe that while he was still in Stratford, William joined a company of actors formed by the Earl of Worcester. He then joined another company called the Admiral's men. It was owned by Lord Howard of Effingham, who was Lord High Admiral of England.

◄ A portrait of the famous Elizabethan actor-manager Edward Alleyn. He was one of the most popular actors of the time.

William was with the Admiral's men when he arrived in London and they often performed at the Rose Theatre. By the early 1590s he had joined another company, called the Chamberlain's men. Their **patron** was Lord Hunsdon, a cousin of Elizabeth I, who was Lord Chamberlain of England.

Actor-playwright

By the time William reached London he would have finished his **apprenticeship** and he would have been a fully fledged actor himself.

In those days it was normal for experienced actors to help in the writing of the plays they were to perform, or to change them as they went along during rehearsals. In this way, William probably started writing. His writing gradually took up more of his time and the acting less, and by the time he reached London he was writing his own plays.

▶ Henry Carey (Lord Hunsdon) was Queen Elizabeth's cousin. He was one of the most powerful men in the kingdom.

Companies of actors

Acting companies had to have a patron, a rich person who supported them financially. They also had actor-managers who were in charge of all the other actors and the performances. A famous actor called Richard Burbage led the Chamberlain's men, while another called Edward Alleyn was in charge of the **rival** Admiral's men.

Live performances

A trip to the theatre in William Shakespeare's time was a very special occasion. Of course, there were no cinemas or televisions in those days, and so it was probably a bit like watching a film and a football match all rolled into one. There was always lots of noise and excitement, and audiences could get so carried away that sometimes people even jumped up and actually joined the actors on the stage!

Buying tickets

When William moved to London, plays were usually performed in the daytime, when it was still light, not in the evening as they are today. A seat under a covered part of the theatre would cost twopence, while for one penny you could stand near the stage. At this time the basic weekly wage was one shilling (twelve pence). The most expensive seats were in the balconies round the sides of the theatre, and those cost sixpence.

Before a play started, there would be lots of chatter and laughter amongst the audience. Boys and girls went round selling drinks, fruit and nuts which people would eat during the performance and sometimes throw at the actors! With so many people crowded into the theatre, pickpockets wandered among the audience to see what they could steal.

▶ This is a portrait of Richard Burbage, one of the greatest actors in Elizabethan times. He was also the manager of the Chamberlain's men.

The play begins

Apprentice actors would announce the start of the play with a great drum roll and trumpet blasts. The actors would then come on to the stage through a door at the back, often dressed in rich, colourful costumes.

Favourite actors would be cheered by the audience when they came on, while unpopular ones, or actors who were considered not to be good, were booed and hissed and had fruit and vegetables thrown at them. In one of William's plays, called *As You Like It*, one of the characters says the words: 'All the world's a stage ...' William believed that even in our everyday lives we are still acting out parts.

▲ The Swan Theatre was the largest theatre in London, and Shakespeare's plays were often performed there. This drawing shows the theatre in the 17th century.

London's theatres

The first London theatre opened in 1567 and was called the Red Lion. The Rose, where William and his company first performed, opened in 1587. The enormous Swan Theatre, which could hold as many as 3000 people, opened eight years later in 1595. Theatres were usually built with wood and plaster walls and with roofs thatched in straw. This is one reason why they did not survive.

Poetry and plays

In William Shakespeare's time, poetry was considered to be the highest and most elegant form of writing. Every educated person in those days was expected to try their hand at writing poems. William probably started writing poems before he wrote any of his plays.

Early plays

No one is certain exactly when William wrote his first play. However, he probably started as a **playwright** by rewriting other people's plays. The first play he wrote himself was probably *Titus Andronicus*, written in about 1590, just before or after he arrived in London. This had a terribly bloodthirsty story, but it was so popular that people flocked to see it. Between the years 1591 and 1593, William wrote the three parts of a history play called *Henry VI* and another called *Richard III*. They were a great success and were performed over and over again in the first year alone.

▲ **This is a woodcut engraving of the Elizabethan actor Will Kempe, shown dancing. He acted with the Chamberlain's men until 1599.**

▲ Royal Shakespeare Company actors Michael Maloney and Clare Holman star in a 1992 production of *Romeo and Juliet*.

Love poems

Although William probably started writing poetry before he wrote plays, his first major poem was not published until 1593. It is called *Venus and Adonis* and is based on an ancient Roman love story. This poem may originally have been written the year before, in 1592. In that year all the theatres in London were closed due to an outbreak of the **plague**. They were closed for nearly two years, and William probably took the opportunity to spend more time with his family in Stratford.

William also wrote many beautiful, short love poems known as sonnets. In one of these, he writes about someone's great beauty:
'Shall I compare thee to a summer's day?
Thou art more lovely and more **temperate**.'

Different kinds of plays

William's plays have been divided into four main kinds: tragedies, comedies, tragicomedies and history plays. A tragedy ends in the death of one or more of the main characters, such as *King Lear*. Comedies usually have happy endings and are often love stories, for example *A Midsummer Night's Dream*. A tragicomedy is a mixture of both tragedy and comedy, such as *The Winter's Tale*. The history plays tell the stories of real events in the past, of great kings and leaders, for example *Henry V* or *Richard III*.

Fame and fortune

From the early 1590s on, William was becoming more and more famous. However, even though his plays were in such demand and the people of London looked forward to each new one, he carried on acting with the Chamberlain's men whenever he had the time.

At the queen's palace

By 1594, the **plague** had ended and the theatres could open again. The Chamberlain's men usually acted at The Theatre or The Rose. By now William had won the **patronage** of a rich **noble** called the Earl of Southampton. The earl's power and influence at the royal **court** brought William to the attention of Elizabeth I, and the Chamberlain's men were asked to act for the queen at her palace in Whitehall.

Family visits

In 1597, William was 33 years old. By now he had written some of his greatest plays, such as *A Midsummer Night's Dream* and *Romeo and Juliet*. His plays were so successful that he was a rich man. Over the years he had been sending money back to his family and had managed to pay off his father's **debts**. Now he could afford to buy them a large, comfortable house in Stratford, called New Place. Although he had been living in London for about seven years, he had made visits to see his wife and children. He usually went during the religious holiday of **Lent**, when all acting was banned and the theatres closed. A family tragedy had happened in 1596, when his son Hamnet died aged only eleven.

◀ Ben Jonson was a famous actor and playwright in Shakespeare's time.

A new theatre

In 1599, The Theatre was closed down permanently and the Chamberlain's men were left without a home. They decided to build a new theatre of their own, south of the River Thames in an area called Southwark. It was named The Globe and it quickly became one of the most popular and successful theatres in London. William was one of the owners and he was to make a lot of money out of it. In *The Tempest*, one of the characters talks about 'the great globe itself', which is a reference to the new theatre.

▲ The modern Globe Theatre in London is a close replica of the original. It was opened in the 1990s and is used for performances of Shakespeare's plays.

Other playwrights

William was not the only successful **playwright** at that time. There were a number of others whose plays were just as popular. Thomas Kyd (1558–94) started a fashion for terrifying plays called revenge tragedies. Christopher Marlowe (1564–93) was the same age as William and also his greatest **rival**. Ben Jonson (1572–1637) was another popular playwright and a friend of William's.

A royal favourite

In 1603, Elizabeth I died. She was succeeded on the throne by her cousin, King James VI of Scotland, who now became James I of England. Like Elizabeth I, he also enjoyed watching plays, and he especially enjoyed the performances of the Chamberlain's men. In fact, he liked them so much that he became their **patron** and the company changed its name to the King's men in his honour.

In demand

William wrote one of the most famous of all his plays for King James. This was the tragedy called *Macbeth*. The story is set in Scotland and celebrates the king's Scottish **ancestors**.

By now, performances by the King's men were in such demand that the company had to take over another theatre, called the Blackfriars Theatre. Even so, William was beginning to spend more time with his family in Stratford.

◄ This portrait of King James VI/I was painted in 1621. James was extremely well-educated and loved watching Shakespeare's plays.

From 1603 until 1604 the theatres had to be closed once more when the **plague** struck London. William probably spent much of the time with his family. During these years, William wrote two more plays, one called *Measure for Measure* and the other *King Lear*, which is one of the greatest of all his plays. In 1607, his elder daughter Susanna married a Stratford doctor called John Hall, and they moved into a house not far from her parents. The following year Susanna gave birth to a baby girl named Elizabeth. A few months later, William's mother Mary died.

The end of a chapter

In 1613, disaster struck. During a performance of William's play *Henry VIII* at The Globe, a spark from a cannon set fire to the thatched roof of the theatre. Fire spread all over the wooden building and it quickly burned down, but the company was not to be defeated. A new Globe theatre with a tiled roof was soon being built, and it opened exactly one year later. However, this accident marked the end of a chapter in William's life – it was time to go home.

▶ **This modern production of *Macbeth* was performed at a theatre in London.**

Another actor in the family

Some people believe that William's youngest brother, Edmund Shakespeare, was also an actor. There are no surviving records of him working in the theatre, but on his gravestone in St Saviour's Church in Southwark, London, he is referred to as 'Edmund Shakespeare, a player'. He may have acted in some of his famous older brother's plays.

Back at home

When William moved back to Stratford in 1613, he had been living and working in London for more than 20 years. He was now 49 years old, which was quite an age in those days. He was to spend his retirement at New Place, the impressive house he had bought some years before.

Family and friends

By now William had stopped writing plays and had handed over this task to younger **playwrights**, such as John Fletcher and Francis Beaumont. It is possible, however, that he continued to act in a few performances.

This was a time of sadness. William's two brothers Gilbert and Richard died within a year of each other. But there were times of happiness, too, as William watched his granddaughter Elizabeth growing up. In February 1616, his younger daughter Judith married Thomas Quiney. William's friends in London, such as Ben Jonson, often came to visit him at New Place. In one of his plays, called *As You Like It*, William wrote the line: 'When I was at home I was in a better place.'

◀ This is a drawing of New Place, the house in Stratford that Shakespeare bought for his family. It was destroyed in 1759 by its then owner who was upset by the number of 'tourists' already coming to look at Shakespeare's last house.

Sick with fever

Early in 1616, William was taken ill with fever. Some historians believe that he had a deadly disease called typhoid. Towards the end of March, his health got much worse. He had to stay in bed and the doctors made him drink water as often as possible.

On 23 April 1616, at the age of 52, William Shakespeare died. He was buried two days later in Holy Trinity Church, where he had been **baptized** exactly 52 years earlier and where other members of his family lay buried.

▶ **This memorial to William Shakespeare can be found in Holy Trinity Church, Stratford, where he is buried.**

Elizabethan gardens

William had the gardens at New Place landscaped and planted with new flowers. Elizabethan gardens were very beautiful, with lots of paths lined with rose bushes and other flowers, and beds planted with sweet-smelling herbs. Many of the plants were used in cooking and to make medicines. You can still visit the gardens today and see the remaining foundations of New Place.

Shakespeare's gift to the world

William left his land and property to be divided between his wife and daughters, most going to Susanna. He left a number of small gifts to friends and cousins and also some money to be given to the poor people of Stratford. William left most of his plays and poems to Susanna.

His work lives on

Undoubtedly some of William Shakespeare's works have been lost and so are unknown to us today. But many have survived, largely because they have always been so popular. As his friend and fellow **playwright** Ben Jonson wrote of William: 'He was not of an age, but for all time!'

After Shakespeare died, two actors in the King's men, called John Heminges and Henry Condell, started putting together a collection of his plays. This was not easy, as many of William's own copies had been lost. But as the two men had acted in many of the plays themselves, they could remember most of the lines and could write them down again. The collection was published in one volume called *Mr William Shakespeare's Comedies, Histories, & Tragedies*. This book is known as the First Folio.

Mr. WILLIAM
SHAKESPEARES
COMEDIES,
HISTORIES, &
TRAGEDIES.

Published according to the True Originall Copies.

LONDON
Printed by Isaac Iaggard, and Ed. Blount. 1623.

▲ The title page of the First Folio, published in 1623. The portrait is of William Shakespeare.

Shakespeare's influence

The influence of William Shakespeare has spread all over the world. His plays and poems have been translated into many different languages and are performed in theatres, on radio and on television. Many have been made into films. In fact, his plays were made into some of the first **silent films**, soon after the invention of cinema.

William's contribution goes far beyond his own work. Over the years since his death, he has inspired not only other playwrights, but also musical composers, painters and even cartoonists to create their own works of art. His voice speaks for all of us and for all time. It is this that makes him one of the greatest writers who has ever lived.

◀ The famous 20th-century actor, Laurence Olivier, in the leading role in Shakespeare's famous play, *Hamlet*.

Glossary

alderman senior local government official

ancestor person from whom someone else is directly descended

apprentice someone who works for a skilled or qualified person in order to learn a trade

bacteria microscopic living things, some are harmful

bailiff the leading local government official, roughly the same as the mayor of a town today

baptize in the Christian religion, to sprinkle holy water on someone to welcome them into the Church

Catholic member of the Roman Catholic Church, one of the main branches of the Christian religion, headed by the Pope in Rome

company of actors group of professional actors

court home of a king and queen and their household and followers

courtier someone who is a member of the royal court

debt owing money to someone

Elizabethan age the years of the reign of Queen Elizabeth I (1558–1603)

folklore tradition of stories and songs, usually of country people

infect pass a disease on to someone else

Latin language of the ancient Romans

Lent in Christian religion, the period of 40 days before Easter when people fast (stop eating certain foods), to remember Jesus' fasting in the wilderness

merchant someone who buys and sells goods

navigator person who explores by ship

noble member of the ruling class, often with an inherited title

patron person who supports an artist such as an actor, painter or writer, or a scholar or explorer

patronage support given by a patron

plague highly infectious disease that can quickly kill people

playwright person who writes plays

Protestant member of the Protestant branch of the Christian Church, which broke away from the Catholic branch in the 16th century

rival competing person or group

silent film the first sort of cinema film, which had no sound

superstition belief that is often based on ignorance or fear

temperate mild

tutor teacher, usually instructing individual pupils

Timeline

1564	William Shakespeare is born
1582	William Shakespeare marries Anne Hathaway
1583	Their daughter Susanna is born
1585	Their twins Hamnet and Judith are born
1590	Shakespeare lives in London from about this time
1591–93	Shakespeare writes *Henry VI* and *Richard III*
1592–94	London's theatres are closed due to the plague
1593	Shakespeare publishes his first major poem, *Venus and Adonis*
1595–96	Shakespeare writes *Romeo and Juliet* and other famous plays
1596	Hamnet Shakespeare dies, aged eleven
circa 1597–99	Shakespeare writes *Much Ado About Nothing, Henry V*
1599	The Globe theatre is opened
1599–1600	Shakespeare writes *As You Like It, Julius Caesar*
1602–3	Shakespeare writes *Othello, All's Well That Ends Well*
1603	Queen Elizabeth I dies
circa 1604–7	Shakespeare writes *King Lear, Macbeth, Antony and Cleopatra*
1611–12	Shakespeare writes *The Tempest*
1613	Shakespeare moves back to Stratford permanently
1616	William Shakespeare dies

Further reading & websites

Visiting the Past: Shakespeare's Birthplace, Jane Shuter (Heinemann Library, 2002)

William Shakespeare, Nina Morgan (Wayland, 1998)

William Shakespeare, Stewart Ross (Evans, 1999)

www.bartleby.com/70/index.html – Oxford edition of the complete works of Shakespeare

daphne.palomar.edu/shakespeare – All you need to know about Shakespeare

Heinemann Explore – an online resource from Heinemann. For Key Stage 2 history go to *www.heinemannexplore.co.uk*

Places to visit

Stratford-upon-Avon, Warwickshire

The Globe Theatre, Bankside, London

Index